The elegies of Tibullus : being the consolations of a Roman lover, done in English verse

Tibullus Tibullus, Theodore Chickering Williams

THE CONSOLATIONS OF A ROMAN LOVER

THE EPIGRAM OF DOMITIUS MARSUS

Tibullus, thee with Virgil, in your prime,
  Death, heedless, to Elysian realms leads down:
That none might longer of lost loves complain,
  Nor warring kings with epic numbers crown.

TO THE GOSSIPS

Rumor avers: "Thy love deceives again."
  Oh, that my ears were deaf, and I at peace!
Such charges leave me wounded and in pain.
  Why scourge a bleeding wretch? Fierce Rumor,
      cease!

The Elegies of Tibullus

BEING

The Consolations of a Roman Lover

Done in English Verse by

THEODORE C. WILLIAMS

ARTI et VERITATI

BOSTON
RICHARD G. BADGER
The Gorham Press
MCMV

Printed at
THE GORHAM PRESS
Boston, U. S. A.

TO WILLIAM COE COLLAR
HEAD MASTER OF THE
ROXBURY LATIN SCHOOL

Our old master ever young to his old boys:

Did Mentor with his mantle thee invest,
Or Chiron lend thee his persuasive lyre,
Or Socrates, of pedagogues the best,
Teach thee the harp-strings of a youth's desir

PREFACE

ALBIUS TIBULLUS was a Roman gentleman, whose father fought on Pompey's side. The precise dates of his birth and death are in doubt, and what we know of his life is all in his own poems; except that Horace condoles with him about Glycera, and Apuleius says Delia's real name was Plautia.

Horace paid him this immortal compliment: *(Epist. 4 bk. 1).*

"Albi nostrorum sermonum candide judex,
"Non tu corpus eras sine pectore; Di tibi formam,
"Di tibi divitias dederant, artemque fruendi."

After his death, Ovid wrote him a fine elegy (p. 115); and Domitius Marsus a neat epigram. The former promised him an immortality equal to Homer's; the latter sent him to Elysium at Virgil's side. These excessive eulogies are the more remarkable in that Tibullus stood, proudly or indolently, aloof from the court. He never flatters Augustus nor mentions his name. He scoffs at riches, glory and war, wanting nothing but to triumph as a lover. Ovid dares to group him with the laurelled shades of Catullus and Gallus, of whom the former had lampooned the divine Julius and the latter had been exiled by Augustus.

But in spite of this contemporary *succès d'estime,* Tibullus is clearly a minor poet. He expresses only one aspect of his time. His few themes are oft-repeated and in monotonous rhythms. He sings of nothing greater than his own lost loves. Yet of

Delia, Nemesis and Neaera, we learn only that all were fair, faithless and venal. For a man whose ideal of love was life-long fidelity, he was tragically unsuccessful.

If this were all, his verse would have perished with that of Macer and Gallus. But it is not all. These love-poems of a private gentleman of the Augustan time, show a delicacy of sentiment almost modern. Of the ribald curses which Catullus hurls after his departing Lesbia, there is nothing. He throws the blame on others: and if, just to frighten, he describes the wretched old age of the girls who never were faithful, it is with a playful tone and hoping such bad luck will never befall any sweet-heart of his. This delicacy and tenderness, with the playful accent, are, perhaps, Tibullus' distinctive charm.

His popularity in 18th century France was very great. The current English version, Grainger's (1755), with its cheap verse and common-place gallantries, is a stupid echo of the French feeling for Tibullus as an erotic poet. Much better is the witty prose version by the elder Mirabeau, done during the Terror, in the prison at Vincennes, and published after his release, with a ravishing portrait of "Sophie," surrounded by Cupids and billing doves. One of the old Parisian editors dared to say:

"Tous ceux qui aiment, ou qui ont jamais aimé, savent par coeur ce délicieux Tibulle."

But it was unjust to classify Tibullus merely as an erotic poet. The gallants of the *ancien régime* were quite capable of writing their own valentines. Tibullus was popular as a sort of Latin Rousseau. He satirized rank, riches and glory as corrupting man's primitive simplicity. He pled for a return to nature, to country-side, thatched cottages, ploughed fields, flocks, harvests, vintages and rustic holidays. He made this plea, not with an armoury of Greek learning, such as cumber Virgil and Horace, but with an original passion. He cannot speak of the jewelled Roman coquettes without a sigh for those happy times when Phoebus himself tended cattle and lived on curds and whey, all for the love of a king's daughter.

For our own generation Tibullus has another claim to notice. All Augustan writers express their dread and weariness of war. But Tibullus protests as a survivor of the lost cause. He has been, himself, a soldier-lover maddened by separation. As an heir of the old order, he saw how vulgar and mercenary was this *parvenu* imperial glory, won at the expense of lost liberties and broken hearts. War, he says, is only the strife of robbers. Its motive is the spoils. It happens because beautiful women want emeralds, Indian slaves and glimmering silk from Cos. Therefore, of course, we fight. But if Neaera and her kind would eat acorns, as of old, we could burn the navies and build cities without walls.

He was indeed a minor poet. He does not carry forward, like Virgil, the whole heritage from the Greeks, or rise like him to idealizing the master-passion of his own age, that vision of a cosmopolitan world-state, centred at Rome and based upon eternal decrees of Fate and Jove. But neither was he duped, as Virgil was, into mistaking the blood-bought empire of the Caesars for the return of Saturn's reign. Sometimes a minor poet, just by reason of his aloofness from the social trend of his time, may also escape its limitations, and sound some notes which remain forever true to what is unchanging in the human heart. I believe Tibullus has done so.

This translation has been done in the play-time of many busy years. I have used what few helps I could find, especially the Mirabeau, above alluded to. The text is often doubtful. But in so rambling a writer it has not seemed to me that the laborious transpositions of later German editors were important. I have rejected as probably spurious all of the fourth book but two short pieces. While I agree with those who find the third book doubtful, I have included it.

But from scholars I must ask indulgence. I have translated with latitude, considering whole phrases rather than single words. But I have always been faithful to the thought and spirit of the original, except in the few passages where euphemism was required. If the reader who has no Latin, gets a pleasing impression of Tibullus, that is what I have chiefly hoped to do. In my forth-coming translations of the *Aeneid* I have kept stricter watch upon verbal accuracy, as is due to an author better-known and more to be revered.

THEODORE C. WILLIAMS.

New York, 1905.

CONTENTS

BOOK I

BOOK II

CONTENTS

BOOK III

BOOK IV

BOOK I

Elegy the First

THE SIMPLE LIFE

Give, if thou wilt, for gold a life of toil!
  Let endless acres claim thy care!
While sounds of war thy fearful slumbers spoil,
  And far-off trumpets scare!

To me my poverty brings tranquil hours;
  My lowly hearth-stone cheerly shines;
My modest garden bears me fruit and flowers,
  And plenteous native wines.

I set my tender vines with timely skill,
  Or pluck large apples from the bough;
Or goad my lazy steers to work my will,
  Or guide my own rude plough.

Full tenderly upon my breast I bear
  A lamb or small kid gone astray;
And yearly worship with my swains prepare,
  The shepherd's ancient way.

BOOK I ELEGY I

I love those rude shrines in a lonely field
  Where rustic faith the god reveres,
Or flower-crowned cross-road mile-stones, half concealed
  By gifts of travellers.

Whatever fruit the kindly seasons show,
  Due tribute to our gods I pour;
O'er Ceres' brows the tasseled wheat I throw,
  Or wreathe her temple door.

My plenteous orchards fear no pelf or harm,
  By red Priapus sentinelled;
By his huge sickle's formidable charm
  The bird thieves are dispelled.

With offerings at my hearth, and faithful fires,
  My Lares I revere: not now
As when with greater gifts my wealthier sires
  Performed the hallowing vow.

No herds have I like theirs: I only bring
  One white lamb from my little fold,
While my few bondmen at the altar sing
  Our harvest anthems old.

Gods of my hearth! ye never learned to slight
  A poor man's gift. My bowls of clay
To ye are hallowed by the cleansing rite,
  The best, most ancient way.

BOOK I ELEGY I

If from my sheep the thief, the wolf, be driven,
  If fatter flocks allure them more,
To me the riches to my fathers given
  Kind Heaven need not restore.

My small, sure crop contents me; and the storm
  That pelts my thatch breaks not my rest,
While to my heart I clasp the beauteous form
  Of her it loves the best.

My simple cot brings such secure repose,
  When so companioned I can lie,
That winds of winter and the whirling snows
  Sing me soft lullaby.

This lot be mine! I envy not their gold
  Who rove the furious ocean foam:
A frugal life will all my pleasures hold,
  If love be mine, and home.

Enough I travel, if I steal away
  To sleep at noon-tide by the flow
Of some cool stream. Could India's jewels pay
  For longer absence? No!

Let great Messala vanquish land and sea,
  And deck with spoils his golden hall!
I am myself a conquest, and must be
  My Delia's captive thrall.

BOOK I ELEGY I

Be Delia mine, and Fame may flout and scorn,
  Or brand me with the sluggard's name!
With cheerful hands I'll plant my upland corn,
  And live to laugh at Fame.

If I might hold my Delia to my side,
  The bare ground were a happier bed
Than theirs who, on a couch of silken pride,
  Must mourn for love long dead.

Gilt couch, soft down, slow fountains murmuring
    song—
  These bring no peace. Befooled by words
Was he who, when in love a victor strong,
  Left it for spoils and swords.

For such let sad Cilicia's captives bleed,
  Her citadels his legions hold!
And let him stride his swift, triumphal steed,
  In silvered robes or gold!

These eyes of mine would look on only thee
  In that last hour when light shall fail.
Embrace me, dear, in death! Let thy hand be
  In my cold fingers pale!

With thine own arms my lifeless body lay
  On that cold couch so soon on fire!
Give thy last kisses to my grateful clay,
  And weep beside my pyre!

BOOK I ELEGY I

And weep! Ah, me! Thy heart will wear no steel
   Nor be stone-cold that rueful day:
Thy faithful grief may all true lovers feel
   Nor tearless turn away!

Yet ask I not that thou shouldst vex my shade
   With cheek all wan and blighted brow:
But, O, to-day be love's full tribute paid,
   While the swift Fates allow.

Soon Death, with shadow-mantled head, will come,
   Soon palsied age will creep our way,
Bidding love's flatteries at last be dumb,
   Unfit for old and gray.

But light-winged Venus still is smiling fair:
   By night or noon we heed her call;
To pound on midnight doors I still may dare,
   Or brave for love a brawl.

I am a soldier and a captain good
   In love's campaign, and calmly yield
To all who hunger after wounds and blood,
   War's trumpet-echoing field.

Ye toils and triumphs unto glory dear!
   Ye riches home from conquest borne!
If my small fields their wonted harvest bear,
   Both wealth and want I scorn!

Elegy the Second

LOVE AND WITCHCRAFT

Bring larger bowls and give my sorrows wine,
  By heaviest slumbers be my brain possessed!
Soothe my sad brows with Bacchus' gift divine,
  Nor wake me while my hapless passions rest!

For Delia's jealous master at her door
  Has set a watch, and bolts it with stern steel.
May wintry tempests strike it o'er and o'er,
  And amorous Jove crash through with thunder-peal!

My sighs alone, O Door, should pierce thee through,
  Or backward upon soundless hinges turn.
The curses my mad rhymes upon thee threw,—
  Forgive them!—Ah! in my own breast they burn!

May I not move thee to remember now
  How oft, dear Door, thou wert love's place of prayer?
While with fond kiss and supplicating vow,
  I hung thee o'er with many a garland fair?

In vain the prayer! Thine own resolve must break
  Thy prison, Delia, and its guards evade.
Bid them defiance for thy lover's sake!
  Be bold! The brave bring Venus to their aid.

BOOK I ELEGY II

'Tis Venus guides a youth through doors unknown;
'Tis taught of her, a maid with firm-set lips
Steals from her soft couch, silent and alone,
And noiseless to her tryst securely trips.

Her art it is, if with a husband near,
A lady darts a love-lorn look and smile
To one more blest; but languid sloth and fear
Receive not Venus' perfect gift of guile.

Trust Venus, too, t' avert the wretched wrath
Of foot-pad, hungry for thy robe and ring!
So safe and sacred is a lover's path,
That common caution to the winds we fling.

Oft-times I fail the wintry frost to feel,
And drenching rains unheeded round me pour,
If Delia comes at last with mute appeal,
And, finger on her lip, throws wide the door.

Away those lamps! Thou, man or maid, away!
Great Venus wills not that her gifts be scanned.
Ask me no names! Walk lightly there, I pray!
Hold back thy tell-tale torch and curious hand!

Yet fear not! Should some slave our loves behold,
Let him look on, and at his liking stare!
Hereafter not a whisper shall be told;
By all the gods our innocence he'll swear.

Or should one such from prudent silence swerve,
The chatterer who prates of me and thee
Shall learn, too late, why Venus, whom I serve,
Was born of blood upon a storm-swept sea.

Nay, even thy husband will believe no ill.
All this a wondrous witch did tell me true:
One who can guide the stars to work her will,
Or turn a torrent's course her task to do.

Her spells call forth pale spectres from their graves,
And charm bare bones from smoking pyres away:
'Mid trooping ghosts with fearful shriek she raves,
Then sprinkles with new milk, and holds at bay.

She has the power to scatter tempests rude,
And snows in summer at her whisper fall;
The horrid simples by Medea brewed
Are hers; she holds the hounds of Hell in thrall.

For me a charm this potent witch did weave;
Thrice if thou sing, then speak with spittings three,
Thy husband not one witness will believe,
Nor his own eyes, if our embrace they see!

BOOK I ELEGY II

But tempt not others! He will surely spy
  All else,—to me, me only, magic-blind!
And, hark! the hag with drugs, she said, would try
  To heal love's madness and my heart unbind.

One cloudless night, with smoky torch, she burned
  Black victims to her gods of sorcery;
Yet asked I not love's loss, but love returned,
  And would not wish for life, if robbed of thee.

Elegy the Third

SICKNESS AND ABSENCE

Am I abandoned? Does Messala sweep
  Yon wide Aegean wave, not any more
He, nor my mates, remembering where I weep,
  Struck down by fever on this alien shore?

Spare me, dark death! I have no mother here,
  To clasp my relics to her widowed breast;
No sister, to pour forth with hallowing tear
  Assyrian incense where my ashes rest.

Nor Delia, who, before she said adieu,
  Asked omens fair at every potent shrine.
Thrice did the ministrants give blessings true,
  The thrice-cast lot returned the lucky sign.

All promised safe return; but she had fears
  And doubting sorrows, which implored my stay;
While I, though all was ready, dried her tears,
  And found fresh pretext for one more delay.

BOOK I ELEGY III

An evil bird, I cried, did near me flit,
  Or luckless portent thrust my plans aside;
Or Saturn's day, unhallowed and unfit,
  Forbade a journey from my Delia's side.

Full oft, when starting on the fatal track,
  My stumbling feet foretold unhappy hours:
Ah! he who journeys when love calls him back,
  Should know he disobeys celestial powers!

Help me, great Goddess! For thy healing power
  The votive tablets on thy shrine display.
See Delia there outwatch the midnight hour,
  Sitting, white-stoled, until the dawn of day!

Each day her tresses twice she doth unbind,
  And sings, the loveliest of the Pharian band.
O that my fathers' gods this prayer could find!
  Gods of my hearth and of my native land!

How happily men lived when Saturn reigned!
  Ere weary highways crossed the fair young world,
Ere lofty ships the purple seas disdained,
  Their swelling canvas to the winds unfurled!

No roving seaman, from a distant course,
  Filled full of far-fetched wares his frail ship's
    hold:
At home, the strong bull stood unyoked; the horse
  Endured no bridle in the age of gold.

Men's houses had no doors? No firm-set rock
  Marked field from field by niggard masters held.
The very oaks ran honey; the mild flock
  Brought home its swelling udders, uncompelled.

Nor wrath nor war did that blest kingdom know;
  No craft was taught in old Saturnian time,
By which the frowning smith, with blow on blow,
  Could forge the furious sword and so much crime.

Now Jove is king! Now have we carnage foul,
  And wreckful seas, and countless ways to die.
Nay! spare me, Father Jove, for on my soul
  Nor perjury, nor words blaspheming lie.

If longer life I ask of Fate in vain,
  O'er my frail dust this superscription be:—
"Here Death's dark hand TIBULLUS *doth de-
tain,*
  Messala's follower over land and sea!"

Then, since my soul to love did always yield,
  Let Venus guide it the immortal way,
Where dance and song fill all th' Elysian field,
  And music that will never die away.

There many a song-bird with his fellow sails,
  And cheerly carols on the cloudless air;
Each grove breathes incense; all the happy vales
  O'er-run with roses, numberless and fair.

BOOK I ELEGY III

Bright bands of youth with tender maidens stray,
  Led by the love-god all delights to share;
And each fond lover death once snatched away
  Winds an immortal myrtle in his hair.

Far, far from such, the dreadful realms of gloom
  By those black streams of Hades circled round,
Where viper-tressed, fierce ministers of doom,—
  The Furies drive lost souls from bound to bound.

The doors of brass, and dragon-gate of Hell,
  Grim Cerberus guards, and frights the phantoms
    back:
Ixion, who by Juno's beauty fell,
  Gives his frail body to the whirling rack.

Stretched o'er nine roods, lies Tityos accursed,
  The vulture at his vitals feeding slow;
There Tantalus, whose bitter, burning thirst
  The fleeting waters madden as they flow.

There Danaus' daughters Venus' anger feel,
  Filling their urns at Lethe all in vain;—
And there's the wretch who would my Delia steal,
  And wish me absent on a long campaign!

O chaste and true! In thy still house shall sit
  The careful crone who guards thy virtuous bed;
She tells thee tales, and when the lamps are lit,
  Reels from her distaff the unending thread.

BOOK I ELEGY III

Some evening, after tasks too closely plied,
  My Delia, drowsing near the harmless dame,
All sweet surprise, will find me at her side,
  Unheralded, as if from heaven I came.

Then to my arms, in lovely disarray,
  With welcome kiss, thy darling feet will fly!
O happy dream and prayer! O blissful day!
  What golden dawn, at last, shall bring thee nigh?

Elegy the Fourth

THE ARTS OF CONQUEST

"Safe in the shelter of thy garden-bower,
"Priapus, from the harm of suns or snows,
"With beard all shag, and hair that wildly flows,—
"O say! o'er beauteous youth whence comes thy power?
"Naked thou frontest wintry nights and days,
"Naked, no less, to Sirius' burning rays."

So did my song implore the rustic son
Of Bacchus, by his moon-shaped sickle known.

"Comply with beauty's lightest wish," said he,
"Complying love leads best to victory.
"Nor let a furious 'No' thy bosom pain;
"Beauty but slowly can endure a chain.
"Slow Time the rage of lions will o'er-sway,
"And bid them fawn on man. Rough rocks and rude
"In gentle streams Time smoothly wears away;
"And on the vine-clad hills by sunshine wooed,
"The purpling grapes feel Time's secure control;
"In Time, the skies themselves new stars unroll.

"Fear not great oaths! Love's broken oaths are
borne
"Unharmed of heaven o'er every wind and wave.
"Jove is most mild; and he himself hath sworn
"There is no force in vows which lovers rave.
"Falsely by Dian's arrows boldly swear!
"And perjure thee by chaste Minerva's hair!

"Be a prompt wooer, if thou wouldst be wise:
"Time is in flight, and never backward flies.
"How swiftly fades the bloom, the vernal green!
"How swift yon poplar dims its silver sheen!
"Spurning the goal th' Olympian courser flies,
"Then yields to Time his strength, his victories;
"And oft I see sad, fading youth deplore
"Each hour it lost, each pleasure it forbore.
"Serpents each spring look young once more; harsh
Heaven
"To beauteous youth has one brief season given.
"With never-fading youth stern Fate endows
"Phœbus and Bacchus only, and allows
"Full-clustering ringlets on their lovely brows.

"Keep at thy loved one's side, though hour by hour
"The path runs on; though Summer's parching star
"Burn all the fields, or blackest tempests lower,
"Or monitory rainbows threaten far.
"If he would hasten o'er the purple sea,
"Thyself the helmsman or the oarsman be.

"Endure, unmurmuring, each unwelcome toil,
"Nor fear thy unaccustomed hands to spoil.
"If to the hills he goes with huntsman's snare,
"Let thine own back the nets and burden bear.
"Swords would he have? Fence lightly when you meet;
"Expose thy body and compel defeat.
"He will be gracious then, and will not spurn
"Caresses to receive, resist, return.
"He will protest, relent, and half-conspire,
"'And later, all unasked, thy love desire.

"But nay! In these vile times thy skill is vain.
"Beauty and youth are sold for golden gain.
"May he who first taught love to sell and buy,
"In grave accurst, with all his riches lie!

"O beauteous youth, how will ye dare to slight
"The Muse, to whom Pierian streams belong?
"Will ye not smile on poets, and delight,
"More than all golden gifts, in gift of song?
"Did not some song empurple Nisus' hair,
"And bid young Pelops' ivory shoulder glow?
"That youth the Muses praise, is he not fair,
"Long as the stars shall shine or waters flow?

"But he who scorns the Muse, and will for gain
"Surrender his base heart,—let his foul cries
"Pursue the Corybants' infuriate train,
"Through all the cities of the Phrygian plain,—
"Unmanned forever, in foul Phrygian guise!

"But Venus blesses lovers who endear
"Love's quest alone by flattery, by fear,
"By supplication, plaint, and piteous tear."

Such song the god of gardens bade me sing
For Titius; but his fond wife would fling
Such counsel to the winds: "Beware," she cried,
"Trust not fair youth too far. For each one's pride
"Offers alluring charms: one loves to ride
"A gallant horse, and rein him firmly in;
"One cleaves the calm wave with white shoulder
bare;
"One is all courage, and for this looks fair;
"And one's pure, blushing cheeks thy praises win."

Let him obey her! But my precepts wise
Are meant for all whom youthful beauty's eyes
Turn from in scorn. Let each his glory boast!
Mine is, that lovers, when despairing most,
My clients should be called. For them my door
Stands hospitably open evermore.
Philosopher to Venus I shall be,
And throngs of studious youth will learn of me.

Alas! alas! How love has been my bane!
My cunning fails, and all my arts are vain.
Have mercy, fair one, lest my pupils all
Mock me, who point a path in which I fall!

Elegy the Fifth

COUNTRY-LIFE WITH DELIA

With haughty frown I swore I could employ
  Thine absence well. But all my pride is o'er!
Now am I lashed, as when a madcap boy
  Whirls a swift top along the level floor.

Aye! Twist me! Plague me! Never shall I say
  Such boast again. Thy scorn and anger spare!
Spare me!—by all our stolen loves I pray,
  By Venus,—by thy wealth of plaited hair!

Was it not I, when fever laid thee low,
  Whose holy rites and offerings set thee free?
Thrice round thy bed with brimstone did I go,
  While the wise witch sang healing charms for thee.

Lest evil dreams should vex thee, I did bring
  That worshipped wafer by the Vestal given;
Then, with loose robes and linen stole, did sing
  Nine prayers to Hecate 'neath the midnight heaven.

BOOK I ELEGY V

All rites were done! Yet doth a rival hold
My darling, and my futile prayers deride:
For I dreamed madly of a life all gold,
If she were healed,—but Heaven the dream denied.

A pleasant country-seat, whose orchards yield
Sweet fruit to be my Delia's willing care,
While our full corn-crop in the sultry field
Stands ripe and dry! O, but my dreams were fair!

She in the vine-vat will our clusters press,
And tread the rich must with her dancing feet;
She oft my sheep will number, oft caress
Some pretty, prattling slave with kisses sweet.

She offers Pan due tributes of our wealth,
Grapes for the vine, and for a field of corn
Wheat in the ear, or for the sheep-fold's health
Some frugal feast is to his altar borne.

Of all my house let her the mistress be!
I am displaced and give not one command!
Then let Messala come! From each choice tree
Let Delia pluck him fruit with her soft hand!

To serve and please so worshipful a guest,
She spends her utmost art and anxious care;
Asks his least wish, and spreads her dainty best,
Herself the hostess and hand-maiden fair.

BOOK I ELEGY V

Mad hope! The storm-winds bore away that dream
  Far as Armenia's perfume-breathing lords.
Great Venus! Did I at thy shrine blaspheme?
  Am I accursed for rash and impious words?

Had I, polluted, touched some altar pure,
  Or stolen garlands from a temple door—
What prayers and vigils would I not endure,
  And weeping kiss the consecrated floor?

Had I deserved this stroke,—with pious pain
  From shrine to shrine my suppliant knees should
    crawl;
I would to all absolving gods complain,
  And smite my forehead on the marble wall.

Thou who thy gibes at love canst scarce repress,
  Beware! The angry god may strike again!
I knew a youth who laughed at love's distress,
  And bore, when old, the worst that lovers ken.

His poor, thin voice he did compel to woo,
  And curled, for mockery, his scanty hair;
Spied on her door, as slighted lovers do,
  And stopped her maid in any public square.

The forum-loungers thrust him roughly by,
  And spat upon their breasts, such luck to turn:
Have mercy, Venus! Thy true follower I!
  Why wouldst thou, goddess, thine own harvest
    burn!

Elegy the Sixth

A LOVER'S CURSES

I strove with wine my sorrows to efface.
  But wine turned tears was all the drink I knew;
I tried a new, strange lass. Each cold embrace
  Brought my true love to mind, and colder grew.

"I was bewitched" she cried "by shameful charms;"
  And things most vile she vowed she could declare.
Bewitched! 'tis true! but by thy soft white arms,
  Thy lovely brows and lavish golden hair!

Such charms had Thetis, born in Nereid cave,
  Who drives her dolphin-chariot fast and free
To Peleus o'er the smooth Hæmonian wave,
  Love-guided o'er long leagues of azure sea.

Ah me! the magic that dissolves my health
  Is a rich suitor in my mistress' eye,
Whom that vile bawd led to her door by stealth
  And opened it, and bade me pine and die.

BOOK I ELEGY VI

That hag should feed on blood. Her festive bowls
  Should be rank gall: and round her haunted room
Wild, wailing ghosts and monitory owls
  Should flit forever shrieking death and doom.

Made hunger-mad, may she devour the grass
  That grows on graves, and gnaw the bare bones down
Which wolves have left! Stark-naked may she pass,
  Chased by the street-dogs through the taunting town!

My curse comes fast. Unerring signs are seen
  In stars above us. There are gods who still
Protect unhappy lovers: and our Queen
  Venus rains fire on all who slight her will.

O cruel girl! unlearn the wicked art
  Of that rapacious hag! For everywhere
Wealth murders love. But thy poor lover's heart
  Is ever thine, and thou his dearest care.

A poor man clings close to thy lovely side,
  And keeps the crowd off, and thy pathway free;
He hides thee with kind friends, and as his bride
  From thy dull, golden thraldom ransoms thee.

Vain is my song. Her door will not unclose
  For words, but for a hand that knocks with gold.
O fear me, my proud rival, fear thy foes!
  Oft have the wheels of fortune backward rolled!

Elegy the Seventh

A DESPERATE EXPEDIENT

Thou beckonest ever with a face all smiles,
Then, God of Love, thou lookest fierce and pale.
Unfeeling boy! why waste on me such wiles?
What glory if a god o'er man prevails?

Once more thy snares are set. My Delia flies
To steal a night—with whom I cannot tell.
Can I believe when she denies, denies—
I, for whose sake she tricked her lord so well?

By me, alas! those cunning ways were shown
To fool her slaves. My skill I now deplore!
For me she made excuse to sleep alone,
Or silenced the shrill hinges of her door.

"Twas I prescribed what remedies to use
If mutual passion somewhat fiercely play;
If there were tell-tale bite or rosy bruise,
I showed what simples take the scars away.

Hear me! fond husband of the false and fair,
Make me thy guest, and she shall chastely go!
When she makes talk with men I shall take care,
Nor shall she at the wine her bosom show.

BOOK I ELEGY VII

I shall take care she does not nod or smile
To any other, nor her hand imbue
With his fast-flowing wine, that her swift guile
May scribble on the board their rendez-vous.

When she goes out, beware! And if she hie
To Bona Dea, where no males may be,
Straight to the sacred altars follow I,
Who only trust her if my eyes can see.

Oh! oft I pressed that soft hand I adore,
Feigning with some rare ring or seal to play,
And plied thee with strong wine till thou didst snore,
While I, with wine and water, won the day.

I wronged thee, aye! But 'twas not what I meant.
Forgive, for I confess. 'Twas Cupid's spell
O'er-swayed me. Who can foil a god's intent?
Now have I courage all my deeds to tell.

Yes, it was I, unblushing I declare,
At whom thy watch-dog all night long did bay:—
But some-one else now stands insistent there,
Or peers about him and then walks away.

He seems to pass. But soon will backward fare
Alone, and, coughing, at the threshold hide.
What skill hath stolen love! Beware, beware!
Thy boat is drifting on a treacherous tide.

BOOK I ELEGY VII

What worth a lovely wife, if others buy
  Thy treasure, if thy stoutest bolt betrays,
If in thy very arms she breathes a sigh
  For absent joy, and feigns a slight *malaise?*

Give her in charge to me! I will not spare
  A master's whip. Her chain shall constant be.
While thou mayst go abroad and have no care
  Who trims his curls, or flaunts his toga free.

Whatever beaux accost her, all is well!
  Not the least hint of scandal shall be made.
For I will send them far away, to tell
  In some quite distant street their amorous trade.

All this a god decrees; a sibyl wise
  In prophet-song did this to me proclaim;
Who when Bellona kindles in her eyes,
  Fears neither twisted scourge nor scorching flame.

Then with a battle-axe herself will scar
  Her own wild arms, and sprinkle on the ground
Blood, for Bellona's emblems of wild war,
  Swift-flowing from the bosom's gaping wound.

A barb of iron rankles in her breast,
  As thus she chants the god's command to all:
"Oh, spare a beauty by true love possessed,
  Lest some vast after-woe upon thee fall!

"For shouldst thou win her, all thy power will fail,
As from this wound flows forth the fatal gore,
Or as these ashes cast upon the gale,
Are scattered far and kindled never more."

And, O my Delia, the fierce prophetess
Told dreadful things that on thy head should fall:—
I know not what they were—but none the less
I pray my darling may escape them all.

Not for thyself do I forgive thee, no!
'Tis thy sweet mother all my wrath disarms,—
That precious creature, who would come and go,
And lead thee through the darkness to my arms.

Though great the peril, oft the silent dame
Would join our hands together, and all night
Wait watching on the threshold till I came,
Nor ever failed to know my steps aright.

Long be thy life! dear, kind and faithful heart!
Would it were possible my life's whole year
Were at the friendly hearth-stone where thou art!
'Tis for thy sake I hold thy daughter dear.

Be what she will, she is not less thy child.
Oh, teach her to be chaste! Though well she knows
No free-born fillet binds her tresses wild
Nor Roman stole around her ankles flows!

BOOK I ELEGY VII

My lot is servile too. Whate'er I see
  Of beauty brings her to my fevered eye.
If I should be accused of crime, or be
  Dragged up the steep street, by the hair, to die:—

Even then there were no fear that I should lay
  Rude hands on thee my sweet! for if o'erswayed
By such blind frenzy in an evil day,
  I should bewail the hour my hands were made.

Yet would I have thee chaste and constant be,
  Not with a fearful but a faithful heart;
And that in thy fond breast the love of me
  Burn but more fondly when we live apart.

She who was never faithful to a friend
  Will come to age and misery, and wind
With tremulous finger from her distaff's end
  The ever-twisting wool; and she will bind

Upon her moving looms the finished thread,
  Or clean and pick the long skeins white as snow.
And all her fickle gallants when they wed,
  Will say, "That old one well deserves her woe."

Venus from heaven will note her flowing tear:
  "I smile not on the faithless," she will say.
Her curse on others fall! O, Delia dear!
  Let us teach true love to grow old and gray!

Elegy the Eighth

MESSALA

The Fatal Sisters did this day ordain,
Reeling threads no god can rend,
Foretelling to this man should bend
The tribes of Acquitaine;
And 'neath his legions' yoke
Th' impetuous torrent Atur glide subdued.
All was accomplished as the Fates bespoke ;
His triumph then ensued:
The Roman youth, exulting from afar,
Acclaimed his mighty deeds,
And watched the fettered chieftains filing by,
While, drawn by snow-white steeds,
Messala followed on his ivory car,
Laurelled and lifted high!

Not without me this glory and renown!
Let Pyrenees my boast attest!
Tarbella, little mountain-town,
Cold Ocean rolling in the utmost West,
Arar, Garonne, and rushing Rhone,
Will bear me witness due;
And valleys broad the blond Carnutes own,
By Liger darkly blue.

BOOK I ELEGY VIII

I saw the Cydnus flow,
Winding on in ever-tranquil mood,
And from his awful peak, in cloud and snow,
Cold Taurus o'er his wild Cilicians' brood.
I saw through thronged streets unmolested flying
Th' inviolate white dove of Palestine;
I looked on Tyrian towers, by soundless waters lying,
Whence Tyrians first were masters of the brine.
The flooding Nile I knew;
What time hot Sirius glows,
And Egypt's thirsty field the covering deluge knows;
But whence the wonder flows,
O Father Nile! no mortal e'er did view.
Along thy bank not any prayer is made
To Jove for fruitful showers.
On thee they call! Or in sepulchral shade,
The life-reviving, sky-descended powers
Of bright *Osiris* hail,—
While, wildly chanting, the barbaric choir,
With timbrels and strange fire,
Their Memphian bull bewail.

Osiris did the plough bestow,
And first with iron urged the yielding ground.
He taught mankind good seed to throw
In furrows all untried;

He plucked fair fruits the nameless trees did hide:
He first the young vine to its trellis bound,
And with his sounding sickle keen
Shore off the tendrils green.

For him the bursting clusters sweet
Were in the wine-press trod;
Song followed soon, a prompting of the god,
And rhythmic dance of lightly leaping feet.
Of Bacchus the o'er-wearied swain receives
Deliverance from all his pains;
Bacchus gives comfort when a mortal grieves,
And mirth to men in chains.
Not to Osiris toils and tears belong,
But revels and delightful song;
Lightly beckoning loves are thine!
Garlands deck thee, god of wine!
We hear thee coming, with the flute's refrain,
With fruit of ivy on thy forehead bound,
Thy saffron vesture streaming to the ground.
And thou hast garments, too, of Tyrian stain,
When thine ecstatic train
Bear forth thy magic ark to mysteries divine.

Immortal guest, our games and pageant share!
Smile on the flowing cup, and hail
With us the *Genius* of this natal day!
From whose anointed, rose-entwisted hair,
Arabian odors waft away.
If thou the festal bless, I will not fail

To burn sweet incense unto him and thee,
And offerings of Arcadian honey bear.

So grant Messala fortunes ever fair!
Of such a sire the children worthy be!
Till generations two and three
Surround his venerated chair!
See, winding upward through the Latin land,
Yon highway past, the Alban citadel,
At great Messala's mandate made,
In fitted stones and firm-set gravel laid,
Thy monument forever more to stand!
The mountain-villager thy fame will tell,
When through the darkness wending late from
 Rome,
He foots it smoothly home.

O Genius of this natal day,
May many a year thy gift declare!
Now bright and fair thy pinions soar away,—
Return, thou bright and fair!

Elegy the Ninth

TO PHOLOE AND MARATHUS

The language of a lover's eyes I cannot choose but see;
The oracles in tender sighs were never dark to me.

No art of augury I need, nor heart of victims slain,
Nor birds of omen singing forth the future's bliss or bane.

Venus herself did round my arm th' enchanted wimple throw,
And taught me—Ah! not unchastised!—what wizardry I know.

Deceive me then no more! The god more furiously burns
Whatever wight rebelliously his first commandment spurns.

To Pholoë

Fair Pholoë! what profits it to plait thy flowing hair?
Why rearrange each lustrous tress with fond, superfluous care?

Why tint that blooming cheek anew? Or give thy fingers, Girl!
To slaves who keep the dainty tips a perfect pink and pearl?

BOOK I ELEGY IX

Why strain thy sandal-string so hard? or why the
daily change
Of mantles, robes, and broideries, of fashions new
and strange?

Howe'er thou hurry from thy glass in careless disarray,
Thou canst not miss the touch that steals thy lover's
heart away!

Thou needst not ask some wicked witch her potion
to provide,
Brewed of the livid, midnight herbs, to draw him to
thy side.

Her magic from a neighbor's field the coming crop
can charm,
Or stop the viper's lifted sting before it work thee
harm.

Such magic would the riding moon from her white
chariot spill,
Did not the brazen cymbals' sound undo the impious
ill!

But fear not thou thy smitten swain of lures and
sorcery tell,
Thy beauty his enchantment was, without inferior
spell.

BOOK I ELEGY IX

To touch thy flesh, to taste thy kiss, his freedom did destroy;
Thy beauteous body in his arms enslaved the hapless boy.

Proud Pholoë! why so unkind, when thy young lover pleads?
Remember Venus can avenge a fair one's heartless deeds!

Nay, nay! no gifts! Go gather them of bald-heads rich and old!
Ay! let them buy thy mocking smiles and languid kisses cold!

Better than gold that youthful bloom of his round, ruddy face,
And beardless lips that mar not thine, however close th' embrace.

If thou above his shoulders broad thy lily arms entwine,
The luxury of monarchs proud is mean compared with thine.

May Venus teach thee how to yield to all thy lover's will,
When blushing passion bursts its bounds and bids thy bosom thrill.

Go, meet his dewy, lingering lips in many a breath-
less kiss!
And let his white neck bear away rose-tokens of his
bliss!

What comfort, girl, can jewels bring, or gems in
priceless store,
To her who sleeps and weeps alone, of young love
wooed no more?

Too late, alas! for love's return, or fleeting youth's
recall,
When on thy head relentless age has cast the silvery pall.

Then beauty will be anxious art,—to tinge the
changing hair,
And hide the record of the years with colors falsely
fair.

To pluck the silver forth, and with strange surgery
and pain,
Half-flay the fading cheek and brow, and bid them
bloom again.

O listen, Pholoë! with thee are youth and jocund
May:
Enjoy to-day! The golden hours are gliding fast
away!

BOOK I ELEGY IX

Why plague our comely Marathus? Thy chaste severity
Let wrinkled wooers feel,—but not, not such a youth as he!

Spare the poor lad! 'tis not some crime his soul is brooding on;
'Tis love of thee that makes his eyes so wild and woe-begone!

He suffers! hark! he moans thy loss in many a doleful sigh,
And from his eyes the glittering tears flow down and will not dry.

"Why say me nay?" he cries, "Why talk of chaperones severe?
I am in love and know the art to trick a listening ear."

"At stolen tryst and *rendez-vous* my breath is light and low,
And I can give a kiss so soft not even the winds may know.

"I creep unheard at dead of night along a marble floor,
"Nor foot-fall make, nor tell-tale creak, when I unbar the door.

"What use are all my arts, if still my lady answers
nay!
"If even to her couch I came, she'd frown and fly
away!

"Or when she says she will, 'tis then she doth most
treacherous prove,
"And keeps me tortured all night long with unre-
warded love.

"And while I say 'She comes, she comes!' whatever
breathes or stirs,
"I think I hear a footstep light of tripping feet like
hers!

"Away vain arts of love! false aids to win the fair!
"Henceforth a cloak of filthy shag shall be my only
wear!

"Her door is shut! She doth deny one moment's in-
terview!
"I'll wear my toga loose no more, as happier lovers
do."

To Marathus

Have done, dear lad! In vain thy tears! She will
not heed thy plea!
Redden no more thy bright young eyes to please her
cruelty!

BOOK I ELEGY IX

To Pholoë

I warn thee, Pholoë, when the gods chastise thy
naughty pride,
No incense burned at holy shrines will turn their
wrath aside.

This Marathus himself, erewhile, made mock of lovers' moan,
Nor knew how soon the vengeful god would mark
him for his own.

He also laughed at sighs and tears, and oft would
make delay,
And oft a lover's fondest wish would baffle and betray.

But now on beauty's haughty ways he looks in fierce
disdain;
He scarce may pass a bolted door without a secret
pain.

Beware, proud girl, some plague will fall, unless thy
pride give way;
Thou wilt in vain the gods implore to send thee
back this day!

Elegy the Tenth

TO VENAL BEAUTY

Why, if my sighs thou wert so soon to scorn,
  Didst dare on Heaven with perjured promise call?
Ah! not unpunished can men be forsworn;
  Silent and slow the perjurer's doom shall fall.

Ye gods, be merciful! Oh! let it be
  That beauteous creatures who for once offend
Your powers divine, for once may go scot-free,
  Escape your scourge, and make some happy end!

'Tis love of gold binds oxen to the plough,
  And bids their goading driver sweat and chide;
The quest of gold allures the ship's frail prow
  O'er wind-swept seas, where stars the wanderers
      guide.

By golden gifts my love was made a slave.
  Oh, that some god a lover's prayer might hear,
And sink such gifts in ashes of a grave,
  Or bid them in swift waters disappear!

BOOK I ELEGY X

But I shall be avenged. Thy lovely grace
  The dust of weary exile will impair;
Fierce, parching suns will mar thy tender face,
  And rude winds rough thy curls and clustering
    hair.

Did I not warn thee never to defile
  Beauty with gold? For every wise man knows
That riches only mantle with a smile
  A thousand sorrows and a host of woes.

If snared by wealth, thou dost at love blaspheme,
  Venus will frown so on thy guilty deed,
'Twere better to be burned or stabbed, I deem,
  Or lashed with twisted scourge till one should
    bleed.

Hope not to cover it! That god will come
  Who lets not mortal secrets safely hide;
That god who bids our slaves be deaf and dumb,
  Then, in their cups, the scandal publish wide.

This god from men asleep compels the cry
  That shouts aloud the thing they last would tell.
How oft with tears I told thee this, when I
  At thy white feet a shameful suppliant fell!

Then wouldst thou vow that never glittering gold
  Nor jewels rare could turn thine eyes from me,
Nor all the wealth Campania's acres hold,
  Nor full Falernian vintage flowing free.

BOOK I ELEGY X

For oaths like thine I would have sworn the skies
  Hold not a star, nor crystal streams look clear:
While thou wouldst weep, and I, unskilled in lies,
  Wiped from thy lovely blush the trickling tear.

Why didst thou so? save that thy fancy strayed
  To beauty fickle as thine own and light?
I let thee go. Myself the torches made,
  And kept thy secret for a live-long night.

Sometimes I led to sudden rendezvous
  The flattered object of thy roving joys.
Mad that I was! Till now I never knew
  How love like thine ensnares and then destroyes.

With wondering mind I versified thy praise;
  But now that Muse with blushes I requite.
May some swift fire consume my moon-struck lays,
  Or flooding rivers drown them out of sight!

And thou, O thou whose beauty is a trade,
  Begone, begone! Thy gains bring cursed ill.
And thou, whose gifts my frail and fair betrayed,
  May thy wife rival thine adulterous skill!

Languid with stolen kisses, may she frown,
  And chastely to thy lips drop down her veil!
May thy proud house be common to the town,
  And many a gallant at thy bed prevail!

BOOK I ELEGY X

Nor let thy gamesome sister e'er be said
   To drain more wine-cups than her lovers be,
Though oft with wine and rose her feast is red
   Till the bright wheels of morn her revels see!

No one like her to pass a furious night
   In varied vices and voluptuous art!
Well did she train thy wife, who fools thee quite,
   And clasps, with practised passion, to her heart!

Is it for thee she binds her beauteous hair,
   Or in long toilets combs each dainty tress?
For thee, that golden armlet rich and rare,
   Or Tyrian robes that her soft bosom press?

Nay, not for thee! some lover young and trim
   Compels her passion to allure his flame
By all the arts of beauty. 'Tis for him
   She wastes thy wealth and brings thy house to shame.

I praise her for it. What nice girl could bear
   Thy gouty body and old dotard smile?
Yet unto thee did my lost love repair—
   O Venus! a wild beast were not so vile!

Didst thou make traffic of my fond caress,
   And with another mock my kiss for gain?
Go, weep! Another shall my heart possess,
   And sway the kingdom where thou once didst reign.

BOOK I ELEGY X

Go, weep! But I shall laugh. At Venus' door
I hang a wreath of palm enwrought with gold;
And graven on that garland evermore,
Her votaries shall read this story told:

"Tibullus, from a lying love set free,
O Goddess, brings his gift, and asks new grace of thee."

Elegy the Eleventh

WAR IS A CRIME

Whoe'er first forged the terror-striking sword,
His own fierce heart had tempered like its blade.
What slaughter followed! Ah! what conflict wild!
What swifter journeys unto darksome death!
But blame not him! Ourselves have madly turned
On one another's breasts that cunning edge
Wherewith he meant mere blood of beast to spill.

Gold makes our crime. No need for plundering
war,
When bowls of beech-wood held the frugal feast.
No citadel was seen nor moated wall;
The shepherd chief led home his motley flock,
And slumbered free from care. Would I had lived
In that good, golden time; nor e'er had known
A mob in arms arrayed; nor felt my heart
Throb to the trumpet's call! Now to the wars
I must away, where haply some chance foe
Bears now the blade my naked side shall feel.
Save me, dear Lares of my hearth and home!
Ye oft my childish steps did guard and bless,
As timidly beneath your seat they strayed.

BOOK I ELEGY XI

Deem it no shame that hewn of ancient oak
Your simple emblems in my dwelling stand!
For so the pious generations gone
Revered your powers, and with offerings rude
To rough-hewn gods in narrow-built abodes,
Lived beautiful and honorable lives.
Did they not bring to crown your hallowed brows
Garlands of ripest corn, or pour new wine
In pure libation on the thirsty ground?
Oft on some votive day the father brought
The consecrated loaf, and close behind
His little daughter in her virgin palm
Bore honey bright as gold. O powers benign!
To ye once more a faithful servant prays
For safety! Let the deadly brazen spear
Pass harmless o'er my head! and I will slay
For sacrifice, with many a thankful song,
A swine and all her brood, while I, the priest,
Bearing the votive basket myrtle-bound,
Walk clothed in white, with myrtle in my hair.

Grant me but this! and he who can may prove
Mighty in arms and by the grace of Mars
Lay chieftains low; and let him tell the tale
To me who drink his health, while on the board
His wine-dipped finger draws, line after line,
Just how his trenches ranged! What madness dire
Bids men go foraging for death in war?
Our death is always near, and hour by hour,
With soundless step a little nearer draws.

What harvest down below, or vineyard green?
There Cerberus howls, and o'er the Stygian flood
The dark ship goes; while on the clouded shore
With hollow cheek and tresses lustreless,
Wanders the ghostly throng. O happier far
Some white-haired sire, among his children dear,
Beneath a lowly thatch! His sturdy son
Shepherds the young rams; he, his gentle ewes;
And oft at eve, his willing labor done,
His careful wife his weary limbs will bathe
From a full, steaming bowl. Such lot be mine!
So let this head grow gray, while I shall tell,
Repeating oft, the deeds of long ago!
Then may long Peace my country's harvests bless!
Till then, let Peace on all our fields abide!
Bright-vestured Peace, who first beneath their yoke
Led oxen in the plough, who first the vine
Did nourish tenderly, and chose good grapes,
That rare old wine may pass from sire to son!
Peace! who doth keep the plow and harrow bright,
While rust on some forgotten shelf devours
The cruel soldier's useless sword and shield.
From peaceful holiday with mirth and wine
The rustic, not half sober, driveth home
With wife and weans upon the lumbering wain.

But wars by Venus kindled ne'er have done;
The vanquished lass, with tresses rudely torn,
Of doors broke down, and smitten cheek complains;

And he, her victor-lover, weeps to see
How strong were his wild hands. But mocking
Love
Teaches more angry words, and while they rave,
Sits with a smile between! O heart of stone!
O iron heart! that could thy sweetheart strike!
Ye gods avenge her! Is it not enough
To tear her soft robe from her limbs away,
And loose her knotted hair?—Enough, indeed,
To move her tears! Thrice happy is the wight
Whose frown some lovely mistress weeps to see!
But he who gives her blows!—Go, let him bear
A sword and spear! In exile let him be
From Venus' mild domain! Come blessed Peace!
Come, holding forth thy blade of ripened corn!
Fill thy large lap with mellow fruits and fair!

BOOK II

Elegy the First

A RUSTIC HOLIDAY

Give us good omen, friends! To-day we bless
With hallowed rites this dear, ancestral seat.
Let Bacchus his twin horns with clusters dress,
And Ceres clasp her brows with bursting wheat!

To-day no furrows! Both for field and man
Be sacred rest from delving toil and care!
With necks yoke-free, at mangers full of bran,
The tranquil steers shall nought but garlands bear.

Our tasks to-day are heaven's. No maid shall dare
Upon a distaff her deft hands employ.
Let none, too rash, our simple worship share,
Who wrought last eve at Venus' fleeting joy!

The gods claim chastity. Come clad in white,
And lave your palms at some clear fountain's brim!
Then watch the mild lamb at the altar bright,
Yon olive-cinctured choir close-following him!

BOOK II ELEGY I

"Ye Guardian Powers, who bless our native soil,
Far from these acres keep ill luck away!
No withered ears the reaper's task to spoil!
Nor swift wolf on our laggard lambs to prey!"

So shall the master of this happy house
Pile the huge logs upon his blazing floor;
While with kind mirth and neighborly carouse,
His bondsmen build their huts beside his door.

The bliss I pray for has been granted me!
With reverent art observing things divine,
I have explored the omens,—and I see
The Guardian Powers are good to me and mine.

Bring old Falernian from the shadows gray,
And burst my Chian seal! He is disgraced,
Who gets home sober from this festive day,
Or finds his door without a step retraced.

Health to Messala now from all our band!
Drink to each letter of his noble name!
Messala! laurelled from the Gallic land,
Of his grim-bearded sires the last, best fame!

Be with me, thou! inspire a song for me
To sing those gods of woodland, hill and glade,
Without whose arts man's hunger still would be
Only on mast and gathered acorns stayed.

BOOK II ELEGY I

They taught us rough-hewn rafters to prepare,
And clothe low cabins with a roof of green;
They bade fierce bulls the servile yoke to bear;
And wheels to move a wain were theirs, I ween.

Our wild fruit was forgot, when apple-boughs
Bore grafts, and thirsty orchards (art divine!)
Were freshed by ditching; while with sweet carouse
The wine-press flowed, and water wed with wine.

Our fields bore harvests, when the dog-star flame
Bade Summer of her tawny tress be shorn;
From fields of Spring the bees, with busy game,
Stored well their frugal combs the live-long morn.

'Twas some field-tiller from his plough at rest,
First hummed his homely words to numbers true,
Or trilled his pipe of straw in songs addressed
To his blithe woodland gods, with worship due.

Some rustic ruddied with vermilion clay
First led, O Bacchus, thy swift choric throng,
And won for record of thy festal day
Some fold's chief goat, fit meed of frolic song!

It was our rustic boys whose virgin band
New coronals of Spring's sweet flowrets made
For offering to the gods who bless our land,
Which on the Lares' hallowed heads were laid.

BOOK II ELEGY I

Our country-lasses find a pleasing care
In soft, warm wool their snowy flocks have bred;
The distaff, skein and spindle they prepare,
And reel, with firm-set thumb, the faultless thread.

Then following Minerva's heavenly art,
They weave with patient toil some fabric proud;
While at her loom the lass with cheerful heart
Sings songs the sounding shuttle answers loud.

Cupid himself with flocks and herds did pass
His boyhood, and on sheep and horses drew
His erring infant bow; but now, alas!
He is an archer far too swift and true.

Not now dull beasts, but luckless maids engage
His enmity; brave men are brave no more;
Youth's strength he wastes, and drives fond, foolish age
To blush and sigh at scornful beauty's door.

Love-lured, the virgin, guarded and discreet,
Slips by the night-watch at her lover's call,
Feels the dark path-way with her trembling feet,
And gropes with out-spread hands along the wall.

Oh! wretched are the wights this god would harm!
But blest as gods whom Love with smiles will sway!
Come, boy divine! and these dear revels charm—
But fling thy burning brands, far, far away!

BOOK II ELEGY I

Sing to this god, sweet shepherds! Ask aloud
Your flocks' good health; then each, discreetly mute,
His love's!—Nay, scream her name! Yon madcap crowd
Screams louder, to its wry-necked Phrygian flute.

On with the sport! Night's chariot appears:
The stars, her children, follow through the sky:
Dark Sleep comes soon, on wings no mortal hears,
With strange, dim dreams that know not where they fly.

Elegy the Second

A BIRTHDAY WISH

Burn incense now! and round our altars fair
With cheerful vows or sacred silence stand!
To-day Cerinthus' birth our rites declare,
With perfumes from the blest Arabian land.

Let his own Genius to our festal haste,
While fresh-blown flowers his heavenly tresses twine
And balm-anointed brows; so let him taste
Our offered loaf and sweet, unstinted wine!

To thee Cerinthus may his favoring care
Grant every wish! O claim some priceless meed!
Ask a fond wife thy life-long bliss to share—
Nay! This the great gods have long since decreed!

Less than this gift were lordship of wide fields,
Where slow-paced yoke and swain compel the corn;
Less, all rich gems the womb of India yields,
Where the flushed Ocean rims the shores of Morn.

BOOK II ELEGY II

Thy vow is granted! Lo! on pinions bright,
   The Love-god comes, a yellow cincture bearing,
To bind thee ever to thy dear delight,
   In nuptial knot, all other knots outwearing.

When wrinkles delve, and o'er the reverend brow
   Fall silver locks and few, the bond shall be
But more endeared; and thou shalt bless this vow
   O'er children's children smiling at thy knee.

Elegy the Third

MY LADY RUSTICATES

To pleasures of the country-side
  My lady-love is lightly flown;
And now in cities to abide
  Betrays a heart of stone.

Venus herself henceforth will choose
  Only in field and farm to walk,
And Cupid but the language use
  Which plough-boy lovers talk.

O what a ploughman I could be!
  How deep the furrows I would trace,
If while I toiled, I might but see
  My mistress' smiling face!

A farmer true, I'd guide my team
  Of barren steers o'er fruitful lands,
Nor murmur at the noon-day beam,
  Or my soft, blistered hands.

BOOK II ELEGY III

Once fair Apollo fed the flocks
  Of King Admetus, like a swain;
Little availed his flowing locks,
  His lyre was little gain.

No virtuous herb to reach that ill
  His heavenly arts of healing knew;
For love made vain his famous skill,
  And all his art o'er-threw.

Himself his herds afield he drove,
  Or where the cooling waters stray;
Himself the willow baskets wove,
  And strained out curds and whey.

Oft would his heavenly shoulders bear
  A calf adown some pathless place;
And oft Diana met him there,
  And blushed at his disgrace.

O often, if his voice divine
  Echoed the mountain glens along,
Out-burst the loud, audacious kine,
  And bellowing drowned his song.

His tripods prince and people found
  All silent to their troubled cry,
His locks dishevelled and unbound
  Woke fond Latona's sigh.

To see his pale, neglected brow,
And unkempt tresses, once so fair,—
They cried, "O where is Phoebus now?
"His glorious tresses, where?"

"In place of Delos' golden fane,
"Love gives thee but a lowly shed!
"O, where are Delphi and its train?
"The Sibyl, whither fled?"

Happy the days, forever flown,
When even immortal gods could dare
Proudly to serve at Venus' throne,
Nor blushed her chain to wear!

"Irreverent fables!" I am told.
But lovers true these tales receive;
Rather a thousand such they hold,
Than loveless gods believe.

O Ceres, who didst charm away
My Nemesis from life in Rome,
May barren glebe thy pains repay
And scanty harvest come!

A curse upon thy merry trade!
Young Bacchus, giver of the vine!
Thy vine-yards have ensnared a maid
Far sweeter than thy wine.

BOOK II ELEGY III

Let herbs and acorns be our meat!
  Drink good old water! Better so
Than that my fickle beauty's feet
  To those far hills should go!

Did not our sires on acorns feed,
  And love-sick rove o'er hill and dale?
Our furrowed fields they did not need,
  Nor did love's harvest fail.

When passion did their hearts employ,
  And o'er them breathed the blissful hour,
Mild Venus freely found them joy
  In every leafy bower.

No chaperone was there, no door
  Against a lover's sighs to stand.
Delicious age! May Heaven restore
  Its customs to our land!

Nay, take me! In my lady's train
  Some stubborn field I fain would plough
Lay on the lash and clamp the chain!
  I bear them meekly now.

Elegy the Fourth

ON HIS LADY'S AVARICE

A woman's slave am I, and know it well.
  Farewell, my birthright! farewell, liberty!
In wretched slavery and chains I dwell,
  For love's sad captives never are set free.

Whether I smile or curse, love just the same
  Brands me and burns. O, cruel woman, spare!
O would I were a rock, to 'scape this flame
  Far off upon the frosty mountains there!

Would I were flint, to front the tempest's power,
  Wave-buffeted on some wild, wreckful shore!
My sad days bring worse nights, and every hour
  Fills me some cup of gall and brims it o'er.

What use are songs? Her greedy hands disdain
  Apollo's gift. She says some gold is due.
Farewell, ye Muses, I have sung in vain!
  Only in quest of *her* I followed *you*.

I sing no wars; nor how the moon and sun
  In heavenly paths their circling chariots steer.
To win my lady's smiles my numbers run;
  Farewell, ye Muses, if ye fail me here!

BOOK II ELEGY IV

Let deeds of bloody crime now make me bold!
No longer at her bolted door I whine;
But I will find that necessary gold,
Though I steal treasure from some holy shrine.

Venus I first will violate; for she
Compelled my crime, and did my heart enthrall
To beauty that requires a golden fee.
Yes, Venus' shrine shall suffer worst of all.

Curse on that man who finds the emerald green,
And Tyrian purples for our flattered girls!
He makes them greedy. Now they must be seen
In Coan robe and gleaming Red Sea pearls.

It spoils them all. Now bolts and barriers hold
Their doors, and watch-dogs threaten through the dark;
But let the lover overflow with gold,—
All bolts fly back and not a dog will bark.

What God did beauty unto gold degrade,
And mix one bliss with many a woe and shame?
Tears, quarrels, curses were the gifts he made;
And Love bears now a very evil name.

False girl, who dost for riches thrust aside
Love's honest vow, may winds and flames conspire
To wreck thy wealth, while all thy beaux deride
The loss, nor throw one bowl-full on the fire!

BOOK II ELEGY IV

O when dark Death shall be thy final guest,
  No lover true will shed the faithful tear,
Nor bring an offering where thy ashes rest,
  Nor lay one garland on thy lonely bier!

But some warm-hearted lass who loved not gain
  Shall live a hundred years, yet be much mourned;
Her tomb shall be some lover's holiest fane,
  With annual gift of all sad flowers adorned.

"Farewell, true heart!" his trembling lips will say,
  "Let peace untroubled bless thy relics dear!"
Oft will he visit, and departing pray,
  "Light lie this earth on her whose rest is here!"

Nay, it is vain such serious songs to breathe:
  I must be modern, if I would prevail.
How much? Just all my ancestors bequeath?
  Come, Lares! You are advertised for sale.

Let Circe and Medea bring the lees
  Of some foul cup! Let Thessaly prepare
Its direst poison! Bring hippomanes,
  Fierce philtre from the frantic, brooding mare!
For if my mistress mix it with a smile,
I drain a draught a thousand times as vile.

Elegy the Fifth

THE PRIESTHOOD OF APOLLO

Smile, Phoebus, on the youthful priest
Who seeks thy shrine to-day!
With lyre and song attend our feast,
And with imperious finger play
Thy loudly thrilling chords to anthems high!
Come, with temples laurel-bound,
O'er thine own thrice-hallowed ground,
Where incense from our altars meets the sky!
Come radiant and fair,
In golden garb and glorious, clustering hair,
The famous guise in which thou sang'st so well
Of victor Jove, when Saturn's kingdom fell!
The far-off future all is thine!
Thy hallowed augurs can divine
Whate'er dark song the birds of omen sing;
Of augury thou art the king,
And thy wise haruspex finds meaning fit
For what the gods have in the victims writ.
The hoary Sibyl taught of thee
Never sings of Rome untrue,
Chanting forth in measures due
Her mysterious prophecy.

Once she bade Aeneas look
In her all-revealing book,
What time from Trojan shore
His father and his fallen gods he bore.
Doubtful and dark to him was Rome's bright name,
While yet his mournful eyes
Saw Ilium dying and her gods in flame.
Not yet beneath the skies
Had Romulus upreared the weight
Of our Eternal City's wall,
Denied to Remus by unequal fate.
Then lowly cabins small
Possessed the seat of Capitolian Jove;
And, over Palatine, the rustics drove
Their herds afield, where Pan's similitude
Dripped down with milk beneath an ilex tall,
And Pales' image rude
Hewn out by pruning-hook, for worship stood.
The shepherd hung upon the bough
His babbling pipes in payment of a vow,—
The pipe of reeds in lessening order placed,
Knit well with wax from longest unto last.
Where proud Velabrum lies,
A little skiff across the shallows plies;
And oft, to meet her shepherd lover,
The village lass is ferried over
For a woodland holiday:
At night returning o'er the watery way,
She brings a tribute from the fruitful farms—
A cheese, or white lamb, carried in her arms.

BOOK II ELEGY V

The Sibyl

"High-souled Aeneas, brother of light-winged Love,
"Thy pilgrim ships Troy's fallen worship bear.
"To thee the Latin lands are given of Jove,
"And thy far-wandering gods are welcome there.
"Thou thyself shalt have a shrine
"By Numícus' holy wave;
"Be thou its genius strong to bless and save,
"By power divine!

"O'er thy ship's storm-beaten prow
"Victory her wings will spread,
"And, glorious, rest at last above a Trojan head.
"I see Rutulia flaming round me now.
"O barbarous Turnus, I behold thee dead!
"Laurentum rushes on my sight,
"And proud Lavinium's castled height,
"And Alba Longa for thy royal heir.
"Now I see a priestess fair
"Close in Mars' divine embrace.
"Daughter of Ilium, she fled away
"From Vesta's fires, and from her virgin face
"The fillet dropped, and quite unheeded lay;
"Nor shield nor corslet then her hero wore,
"Keeping their stolen tryst by Tiber's sacred shore!
"Browse, ye bulls, along the seven green hills!
"For yet a little while ye may,
"E'er the vast city shall confront the day!
"O Rome! thy destined glory fills

"A wide world subject to thy sway,—
"Wide as all the regions given
"To fruitful Ceres, as she looks from heaven
"O'er her fields of golden corn,
"From the opening gates of morn
"To where the Sun in Ocean's billowy stream
"Cools at eve his spent and panting team.
"Troy herself at last shall praise
"Thee and thy far-wandering ways.
"My song is truth. Thus only I endure
"The bitter laurel-leaf divine,
"And keep me at Apollo's shrine
"A virgin ever pure."

So, Phoebus, in thy name the Sibyl sung,
As o'er her frenzied brow her loosened locks she
flung.

In equal song Heróphile
Chanted forth the times to be,
From her cold Marpesian glade.
Amalthéa, dauntless maid,
In the blessed days gone by,
Bore thy book through Anio's river
And did thy prophecies deliver,
From her mantle, safe and dry.

All prophesied of omens dire,
The comet's monitory fire,
Stones raining down, and tumult in the sky

Of trumpets, swords, and routed chivalry;
The very forests whispered fear,
And through the stormful year
Tears, burning tears, from marble altars ran;
Dumb beast took voice to tell the fate of man;
The Sun himself in light did fail
As if he yoked his car to horses mortal-pale.

Such was the olden time. O Phoebus, now
Of mild, benignant brow,
Let those portents buried be
In the wild, unfathomed sea!
Now let thy laurel loudly flame
On altars to thy gracious name,
And give good omen of a fruitful year
Crackling laurel if the rustic hear,
He knows his granary shall bursting be,
And sweet new wine flow free,
And purple grapes by jolly feet be trod,
Vat and cellar will be too small,
While at the vintage-festival,
With choral song,
The tipsy swains carouse the shepherd's god:
"Away, ye wolves, and do our folds no wrong!"

Then shall the master touch the straw-built fire,
And as it blazes high and higher,
Lightly leap its lucky crest.
A welcome heir with frolic face

Shall his jovial sire embrace,
And kiss him hard and pull him by the ears;
While o'er the cradle the good grand-sire bent
Will babble with the babe in equal merriment,
And feel no more his weight of years.

There in soft shadow of some ancient tree,
Maidens, boys, and wine-cups be,
Scattered on the pleasant grass;
From lip to lip the cups they pass;
Their own mantles garland-bound
Hang o'er-head for canopy,
And every cup with rose is crowned;
Each at banquet buildeth high
Of turf the table, and of turf the bed,—
Such was ancient revelry!
Here too some lover at his darling's head
Flings words of scorn, which by and by
He wildly prays be left unsaid,
And swears that wine-cups lie.

O under Phoebus' ever-peaceful sway,
Away, ye bows, ye arrows fierce, away!
Let Love without a shaft among earth's peoples
stray!
A noble weapon! but when Cupid takes
His arrow,—ah! what mortal wound he makes!
Mine is the chief. This whole year have I lain
Wounded to death, yet cherishing the pain,
And counting my delicious anguish gain.

BOOK II ELEGY V

Of Nemesis my song must tell!
Without her name I make no verses well,
My metres limp and all fine words are vain!

Therefore, my darling, since the powers on high
Protect the poets,—O! a little while
On Apollo's servant smile!
So let me sing in words divine
An ode of triumph for young Messaline.
Before his chariot he shall bear
Towns and towers for trophies proud,
And on his brow the laurel-garland wear;
While, with woodland laurel crowned.
His legions follow him acclaiming loud,
"Io triumphe," with far-echoing sound.

Let my Messala of the festive crowd
Receive applause, and joyfully behold
His son's victorious chariot passing by!

Smile, Phoebus there! Thy flowing locks all gold!
Thy virgin sister, too, stoop with thee from the sky!

Elegy the Sixth

LET LOVERS ALL ENLIST

Now for a soldier Macer goes. Will Cupid take
the field?
Will Love himself enlist, and bear on his soft breast
a shield?

Through weary marches over land, through wandering waves at sea,
Armed *cap-a-pie,* will that small god the hero's comrade be?

O burn him, boy, I pray, that could thy blessed favors slight!
Back to the ranks the straggler bring beneath thy
standard bright!

Yet, if to soldiers thou art kind, I too will volunteer,
I too will from a helmet drink, nor thirst in desert's
fear.

Venus, good-bye! Now, off I go! Good-bye, sweet
ladies all!
I am all valor, and delight to hear the trumpets call.

BOOK II ELEGY VI

Large is my brag! But while with pride my project I recite,
I see her bolted door,—and then my boasting fails me quite.

Never to visit her again, with many an oath I swore;
But while I vowed, my feet had run unguided to her door.

Come now, ye lovers all! who serve in Cupid's hard campaign,
Let us together to the wars, and thus our peace regain!

This age of iron frowns on love and smiles on golden gain,—
On spoils of war which must be won by agony and pain.

For spoils alone our swords are keen, and deadly spears are hurled
While carnage, wrath, and swifter death fly broadcast through the world.

For spoils, with double risk of death the threatening seas we sail,
And climb the steel-beaked ship-of-war, so mighty and so frail!

BOOK II ELEGY VI

The spoilers proud to boundless lands their bloody
titles read,
And see innumerable flocks o'er endless acres feed.

Fine foreign marbles they will bring; and all the
city stare,
While one tall column for a house a thousand oxen
bear.

They bind with bars the tameless sea; behind a
rampart proud
Their little fishes swim in calm, when wintry storms
are loud.

Ah! Love! Will not a Samian bowl hold all our
mirth and wine?
And pottery of poor Cuman clay, with love, seem
fair and fine?

Nay! Woe is me! Naught now but gold can please
our ladies gay;
And so, since Venus asks for wealth, the spoils of
war must pay.

My Nemesis shall roll in wealth; and promenade
the town,
All glittering, with my golden gifts upon her gorge-
ous gown.

BOOK II ELEGY VI

Her filmy web of Coan weave with golden broidery
gleams;
Her swarthy slaves the Indian sun touched with its
burning beams.

In rival hues to make her fair all conquered regions
vie,
Afric its azure must bestow, and Tyre its purple dye.

O look—I tell what all men know—on that most
favored lover!
Once in the market-place he sat, with both his soles
chalked over.

Elegy the Seventh

A VOICE FROM THE TOMB

Death should have ended all my heavy care;
  But Hope, so credulous and fond, would say:
"Yield not thy precious life to this despair!
  "Tomorrow will be happier than today."

Hope feeds the farmer; and confides his seed
  To furrows, till full foison crown his wish;
Hope snares the birds, or with a bending reed
  And little baited hooks, deludes the fish.

Hope sends the slave a song, while his hard task
  He must in clanking fetters captive ply:
Hope tells me Nemesis grants all I ask
  Wilt not? Wouldst make divinest Hope a lie?

Thee by thy sister's ashes I implore,
  Whom death untimely snatched in youth away,
By that blest grave we visit o'er and o'er,
  Where oft my garland wet with tears I lay.

BOOK II ELEGY VII

Thither I fly: and as my sorrow flows
  Unto that voiceless dust my grief confide.
She will not fail to heed her mourner's woes,
  Nor let me plead forever at thy side.

Almost I fear to bid thy heart recite
  How oft she bade thee with my love comply,
Lest in some doleful vision of the night
  Her sweet, forgotten shade should meet thine eye;

Lest at thy couch thy sister, with sad frown,
  Should stand in such dread aspect as she wore
When from that skyward window fallen down,
  She fled, all wounded, to the Stygian shore.

No more! Thy sorrows let me not unseal!
  I am not worth that thou shouldst lose a smile,
Nor that th' expressive light thine eyes reveal
  A single bitter tear-drop should defile.

* * * * * * * *

BOOK III

Elegy the First

THE NEW-YEAR'S GIFT

Now the month of Mars beginning brings the merry season near,
By our fathers named and numbered as the threshold of the year.
Faithfully their custom keeping, through the wide streets to and fro,
Offered at each friendly dwelling, seasonable gifts must go.
O what gifts, Pierian Muses, may acceptably be poured
On my own adored Neaera?—or, if not my own, adored!

Song is love's best gift to beauty; gold but tempts the venal soul;
Therefore, 'tis a song I send her on this amateurish scroll.
Wind a page of saffron parchment round the white papyrus there,
Polish well with careful pumice every silvery margin fair;

BOOK III ELEGY I

On the dainty little cover, for a title to the same,
Let her bright eyes read the blazon of a love-sick poet's name.
Let the pair of horn-tipped handles be embossed with colors gay,
For my book must make a toilet, must put on its best array.

By Castalia's whispering shadow, by Pieria's vocal spring,
By yourselves, O listening Muses, who did prompt the song I sing,—
Fly, I pray you, to her chamber, and my pretty booklet bear,
All unmarred and perfect give it, every color fresh and fair:
Let her send you back, confessing, if our hearts together burn;
Or, if she but loves me little, or will nevermore return.
Utter first, for she deserves it, many a golden wish and vow;
Then deliver this true message, humbly, as I speak it now.

'Tis a gift, O chaste Neaera, from thy husband yet to be.
Take the trifle, though a "brother" now is all he seems to thee.

BOOK III ELEGY I

He will swear he loves thee dearer than the blood
in all his veins;
Whether husband, or if only that cold "sister" name
remains.
Ah! but "wife" he calls it: nothing takes this sweet
hope from his soul!
Till a hapless ghost he wanders where the Stygian
waters roll.

Elegy the Second

HE DIED FOR LOVE

Whoe'er from darling bride her husband dear
  First forced to part, had but a heart of stone;
And not less hard the man who could appear
  To bear such loss and live unloved, alone.

I am but weak in this; such fortitude
  My soul has not; grief breaks my spirit quite.
I shame not to declare it is my mood
  To sicken of a life such sorrows smite.

When I shall journey to the shadowy land,
  And over my white bones black ashes be,
Beside my pyre let fair Neaera stand,
  With long, loose locks unbound, lamenting me.

Let her dear mother's grief with hers have share,
  One mourn a husband, one a son bewail!
Then call upon my ghost with holy prayer,
  And pour ablution o'er their fingers pale.

BOOK III ELEGY II

The white bones, which my body's wreck outlast,
Girdled in flowing black they will upbear,
Sprinkle with rare, old wine, and gently cast
In bath of snowy milk, with pious care.

These will they swathe with linen mantles o'er,
And lay unmouldering in their marble bed;
Then gift of Arab or Panchaian shore,
Assyrian balm and Orient incense shed.

And may they o'er my tomb the gift disburse
Of faithful tears, remembering him below;
For those cold ashes I have made this verse,
That all my doleful way of death may know.

My oft-frequented grave the words shall bear,
And all who pass will read with pitying eyes:—
"Here Lygdamus, consumed with grief and care
"For his lost bride Neaera, hapless lies."

Elegy the Third

RICHES ARE USELESS

'Tis vain to plague the skies with eager prayer,
  And offer incense with thy votive song,
If only thou dost ask for marbles fair,
  To deck thy palace for the gazing throng.

Not wider fields my oxen to employ,
  Nor flowing harvests and abundant land,
I ask of heaven; but for a long life's joy
  With thee, and in old age to clasp thy hand.

If when my season of sweet light is o'er,
  I, carrying nothing, unto Charon yield,
What profits me a ponderous golden store,
  Or that a thousand yoke must plough my field?

What if proud Phrygian columns fill my halls,
  Taenarian, Carystian, and the rest,
Or branching groves adorn my spacious walls,
  Or golden roof, or floor with marbles dressed?

BOOK III ELEGY III

What pleasure in rare Erythraean dyes,
  Or purple pride of Sidon and of Tyre,
Or all that can solicit envious eyes,
  And which the mob of fools so well admire?

Wealth has no power to lift life's load of care,
  Or free man's lot from Fortune's fatal chain;
With thee, Neaera, poverty looks fair,
  And lacking thee, a kingdom were in vain.

O golden day that shall at last restore
  My lost love to my arms! O blest indeed,
And worthy to be hallowed evermore!
  May some kind god my long petition heed!

No! not dominion, nor Pactolian stream,
  Nor all the riches the wide world can give!
These other men may ask. My fondest dream
  Is, poor but free, with my true wife to live.

Saturnian Juno, to all nuptials kind,
  Receive with grace my ever-anxious vow!
Come, Venus, wafted by the Cyprian wind,
  And from thy car of shell smile on me now!

But if the mournful sisters, by whose hands
  Our threads of life are spun, refuse me all—
May Pluto bid me to his dreary lands,
  Where those wide rivers through the darkness
      fall!

Elegy the Fourth

A DREAM FROM PHOEBUS

Be kinder, gods! Let not the dreams come true
  Which last night's cruel slumber bade believe!
Begone! your vain, delusive spells undo,
  Nor ask me to receive!

The gods tell truth. With truth the Tuscan seer
  In entrails dark a book of fate may find;
But dreams are folly and with fruitless fear
  Address the trembling mind.

Although mankind, against night's dark surprise
  With sprinkled meal or salt ward off the ill,
And often turn deaf ear to prophets wise,
  While dreams deceive them still;—

May bright Lucina my foreboding mind
  From such vain terrors of the night redeem,
For in my soul no deed of guilt I find,
  Nor do my lips blaspheme.

BOOK III ELEGY IV

Now had the Night upon her ebon wain
  Passed o'er the upper sky, and dipped a wheel
In the blue sea: but Sleep, the friend of pain,
  Refused my sense to seal.

Sleep stands defeated at the house of care:
  And only when from purpled orient skies
Peered Phoebus forth, did tardy slumber bear
  Down on my weary eyes.

Then seemed a youth with holy laurel crowned
  To fill my door: a wight so wondrous rare
Was not in all the vanished ages found.
  No marble half so fair!

Adown his neck, with myrtle-buds inwove
  And Syrian dews, his unshorn tresses flow:
White is he as the moon in heaven above,
  But rose is blent with snow.

Like that soft blush on face of virgin fair
  Led to her husband; or as maidens twine
Lilies in amaranth; or Autumn's air
  Tinges the apples fine.

A long, loose mantle to his ankles played,—
  Such vesture did his lucent shape enfold:
His left hand bore the vocal lyre, all made
  Of gleaming shell and gold.

BOOK III ELEGY IV

He smote its strings with ivory instrument,
  And words auspicious tuned his heavenly tongue;
Then, while his hands and voice concording blent,
  These sad, sweet words he sung:

"Hail, blest of Heaven! For a poet divine
  Phoebus and Bacchus and the Muses bless.
But Bacchus and the skilful Sisters nine
  No prophecies possess.

"But of what Fate ordains for times to be
  Jove gave me vision. Therefore, minstrel dear!
Receive what my unerring lips decree!
  The Cynthian wisdom hear!

"She whom thy love holds dearer than sweet child
  Is to a mother's breast, or virgin soft
To longing lover, she for whom thy wild
  Prayers vex high Heaven so oft,

"Who worries thee each day, and vainly fills
  Dark-mantled sleep with visions that beguile,
Lovely Neaera, theme of all thy quills,
  Now elsewhere gives her smile.

"For sighs not thine her fickle passions flame:
  For thy chaste house Neaera has no care.
O cruel tribe! O woman, faithless name!
  Curse on the false and fair!

"But woo her still! For mutability
Is woman's soul. Fond vows may yet prevail.
Fierce love bears well a woman's cruelty,
Nor at the lash will quail.

"That I did feed Admetus' heifers white
Is no light tale. Upon the lyric string
Nor more could I my joyful notes indite,
Nor with sweet concord sing.

"On oaten pipe I sued the woodland Muse—
I, of Latona and the Thunderer son!
Thou knowst not what love is, if thou refuse
T'endure a cruel one.

"Go, then, and ply her with persuasive woe!
Soft supplications the hard heart subdue.
Then, if my oracles the future know,
Give her this message true:

" 'The God whose seat is Delos' marble isle,
Declares this marriage happy and secure.
It has Apollo's own auspicious smile.
Cast off that rival wooer!' "

He spoke: dull slumber from my body fell.
Can I believe such perils round me fold?
That such discordant vows thy tongue can tell?
Thy heart in guilt so bold?

BOOK III ELEGY IV

Thou wert not gendered by the Pontic Sea,
  Nor where Chimaera's lips fierce flame out-pour,
Nor of that dog with tongues and foreheads three,
  His back all snakes and gore;

Nor out of Scylla's whelp-engirdled womb;
  Nor wert thou of fell lioness the child;
Nor was thy cradle Scythia's forest-gloom,
  Nor Syrtis' sandy wild.

No, but thy home was human! round its fire
  Sate creatures lovable: of all her kind
Thy mother was the mildest, and thy sire
  Showed a most friendly mind.

May Heaven in these bad dreams good omen show,
And bid warm south-winds to oblivion blow!

Elegy the Fifth

TO FRIENDS AT THE BATHS

You take your pleasure by Etrurian streams,
  Save when the dog-star burns:
Or bathe you where mysterious Baiae steams,
  When purple Spring returns.

But dread Persephone assigns to me
  The hour of gloom and fears.
O Queen of death! be innocence my plea!
  Pity my youthful tears!

I never have profaned that sacred shrine
  Where none but women go,
Nor in my cup cast hemlock, or poured wine
  Death-drugged for friend or foe.

I have not burned a temple: nor to crime
  My fevered passions given:
Nor with wild blasphemy at worship-time
  Insulted frowning Heaven.

BOOK III ELEGY V

Not yet is my dark hair defaced with gray,
  Nor stoop nor staff have I;
For I was born upon that fatal day
  That saw two consuls die.

What profits it from tender vine to tear
  The growing grape? Or who
Would pluck with naughty hand an apple fair,
  Before its season due?

Have mercy! gods who keep the murky stream
  Of that third kingdom dark!
On my far future let Elysium beam!
  Postpone me Charon's bark!—

Till wrinkled age shall make my features pale,
  And to the listening boys
The old man babbles his repeated tale
  Of vanished days and joys!

I trust I fear too much this fever-heat
  Which two long weeks I have,
While with Etrurian nymphs ye sweetly meet,
  And cleave the yielding wave.

Live lucky, friends! live loyal unto me,
  Though life, though death be mine!
Let herds all black dread Pluto's offering be
  With white milk and red wine!

Elegy the Sixth

A FARE-WELL TOAST

Come radiant Bacchus! With the hallowed leaf
Of grape and ivy be thy forehead crowned!
For thou canst chase away or cure my grief—
Let love in wine be drowned!

Dear bearer of my cup, come, brim it o'er!
Pour forth unstinted our Falernian wine!
Care's cruel brood is gone; I toil no more,
If Phoebus o'er me shine.

Dear, jovial friends, let not a lip be dry!
Drink as I drink, and every toast obey!
And him who will not with my wine-cup vie,
May some false lass betray!

This god makes all men rich. He tames proud souls,
And bids them by a woman's hand be chained;
Armenian tigresses his power controls,
And lions tawny-maned.

That love-god is as strong; but I delight
In Bacchus rather. Fill our cups once more!
Just and benign is he, if mortal wight
Him and his vines adore!

But, O! he rages, if his gift ye spurn.
  Drink, if ye dare not a god's anger brave!
How fierce his stroke, let temperate fellows learn
  Of Pentheus' gory grave.

Away such fear! Rather may some fierce stroke
  On that false beauty fall!—O frightful prayer!
O, I am mad! O may my curse be broke,
  And melt in misty air!

For, O Neaera, though I am forgot,
  I ask all gods to bless thee, every one.
Back to my cups I go. This wine has brought
  After long storms, the sun.

Alas! How hard to masque dull grief in joy!
  A sad heart's jest—what bitter mockery!
With vain deceit my laughing lips employ
  Loud mirth that is a lie.

But why complain and moan? O wretched me!
  When will my lagging sorrows haste and go?
Delightful Bacchus at his mystery
  Forbids these words of woe.

Once, by the wave, lone Ariadne pale,
  Abandoned of false Theseus, weeping stood:—
Our wise Catullus tells the doleful tale
  Of love's ingratitude.

BOOK III ELEGY VI

Take warning friends! How fortunate is he,
Who learns of others' loss his own to shun!
Trust not caressing arms and sighs, nor be
By flatteries undone!

Though by her own sweet eyes her oath she swear,
By solemn Juno, or by Venus gay,
At oaths of love Jove laughs, and bids the air
Waft the light things away.

It is but folly, then, to fume and fret,
If one light lass that old deception wrought;
O that I too might evermore forget
To speak my heart's true thought!

O that my long, long nights brought peace and thee!
That nought but thee my waking eyes did fill!
Thou wert most false and cruel, woe is me!
False! But I love thee still.

L'Envoi

How well fresh water mixes with old wine!
Bacchus loves water-nymphs. Bring water, boy!
What care I where she sleeps? This night of mine
Shall I in sighs employ?

Make the cup strong, I tell you! Stronger there!
Wine only! While the Syrian balm o'er-flows!
Long would I revel with anointed hair,
And wear this wreath of rose.

BOOK IV

Elegy the Thirteenth

A LOVER'S OATH

No! ne'er shall rival lure me from thine arms!
(In such sweet bond did our first sighs agree!)
Save for thine own I see no woman's charms;
No maid in all the world is fair but thee.

Would that no eyes but mine could find thee fair!
Displease those others! Save me this annoy!
I ask not envy nor the people's stare:—
Wisest is he who loves with silent joy.

With thee in gloomy woods my life were gay,
Where pathway ne'er was found for human feet.
Thou art my balm of care, in dark my day,
In wildest waste, society complete.

If Heaven should send a goddess to my bed,
All were in vain. My pulse would never rise.
I swear thee this by Juno's holy head —
Greatest to us of all who hold the skies.

What madness this? I give away my case!
Swear a fool's oath! Thy fears my safety won.
Now wilt thou flirt, and tease me to my face,—
Such mischief has my babbling folly done.

Now am I but thy slave: yet thine remain.
My mistress' yoke I never shall undo.
To Venus' altar let me drag my chain!
She brands the proud, and smiles on lovers true.

OVID'S LAMENT FOR TIBULLUS' DEATH

If tears for their dead sons, in deep despair,
  Mothers of Memnon and Achilles shed,
If gods in mortal grief have any share,
  O Muse of tears! bow down thy mournful head!

Tibullus, thy true minstrel and best fame,
  Mere lifeless clay, on tall-built pyre doth blaze;
While Eros, with rent bow, extinguished flame,
  And quiver empty, his wild grief displays.

Behold, he comes with trailing wing forlorn,
  And smites with desperate hands his bosom bare!
Tears rain unheeded o'er his tresses torn,
  And many a trembling sob his soft lips bear.

Thus for a brother Eros mourned of yore,
  Aeneas, in Iulus' regal hall;
Not less do Venus' eyes this death deplore
  Than when she saw her slain Adonis fall.

OVID'S LAMENT

Yet poets are sacred! Simple souls have deemed
That ranked with gods we sons of song may stand.
See one and all by sullen Death blasphemed,
And violated by his shadowy hand!

Little avails it Orpheus that his sire
Was more than man; for though his songs restrain
The wolves of Ismara, his love-lorn lyre
Wails in the wildwood gloom with anguish vain.

Maeonides, from whose exhaustless well
All bards since then some tribute stream derive,—
Him, even him, th' Avernian shades compel;
Only his songs his scattered dust survive

Yet songs endure. Endures the Trojan fame,
And how Penelope's wise nights were passed.
So Nemesis and Delia have a name,—
A poet's earliest passion and his last.

Live piously! Build shrines! Revere the skies!
Death, from the temple, thrusts thee to the tomb!
Or sing divinely! Lo, Tibullus dies!
One scanty urn gives all his ashes room.

Could not that laurelled head the flames restrain?
How dared they that inspired breast explore?
Rather they should have burned some golden fane
Of gods,—of gods who this last insult bore!

OVID'S LAMENT

Yet 'tis my faith the Queen of Love the while,
  Whose altars crown the bright, voluptuous steep
Of Eryx, at that sight did lose her smile;
  Oh! I believe sweet Venus deigned to weep!

But he had feared worse deaths: for now he lies
  Not on Phaeacia's strand in grave unknown;
His own dear mother closed his fading eyes,
  And brought her prayers to bless his votive stone.

Thither drew near in mournful disarray
  His sister pale, her mother's grief to share:
Thither no less, their rival tears to pay,
  His Nemesis and Delia, fond and fair.

There Delia murmured, "In such love as thine
  I was too happy; thou, supremely blest,"
But Nemesis:—"Nay, nay! The loss is mine;
  By mine alone his dying hand was pressed."

If after death, we haply may retain
  More of true being than a name and shade,
Tibullus now the bright Elysian plain
  Doth enter, and hears stir of welcome made.

With ivy garlands on his fadeless brow,
  Catullus hails his peer in perfect rhyme;
Comes Calvus, too; and slandered Gallus! thou,—
  Not guilty, save if wasted love be crime!

OVID'S LAMENT

Such comrades now attend thy happy shade,—
  If shade in truth to our frail flesh belong:
Th' Elysian company is larger made
  By thee, Tibullus, skilled in noble song!

May thy bones rest in peace! is my fond prayer:
  Safe and inviolate thine urn shall be.
Be changeless peace on thy loved relics there!
  And light the hallowed earth that shelters thee!